PRESHUSJUEL ART'S ROOTS

The Most Precious Jewell

Johnanna Barnes

Independently Published

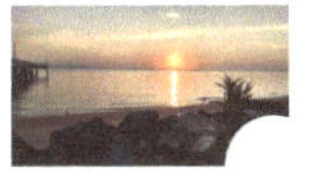

PREFACE

This book is all about my mother and her connection not only to me but my Art and my kids as well. My kids did not get to know their grandmother too well and can only vaguely remeber her in fact. So it was with these thoughts in mind that I worte this book. I wanted not only my three kids to know more about her but anyone else who want to find out more about her and to keep her leagacy alive.

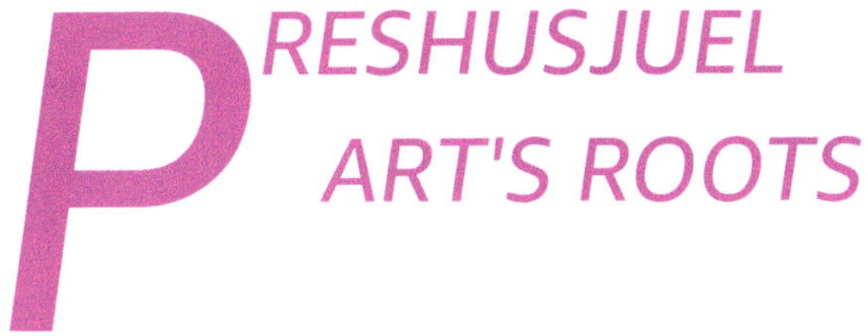PRESHUSJUEL PART'S ROOTS

The Most Precious Jewell

copyright

dedication

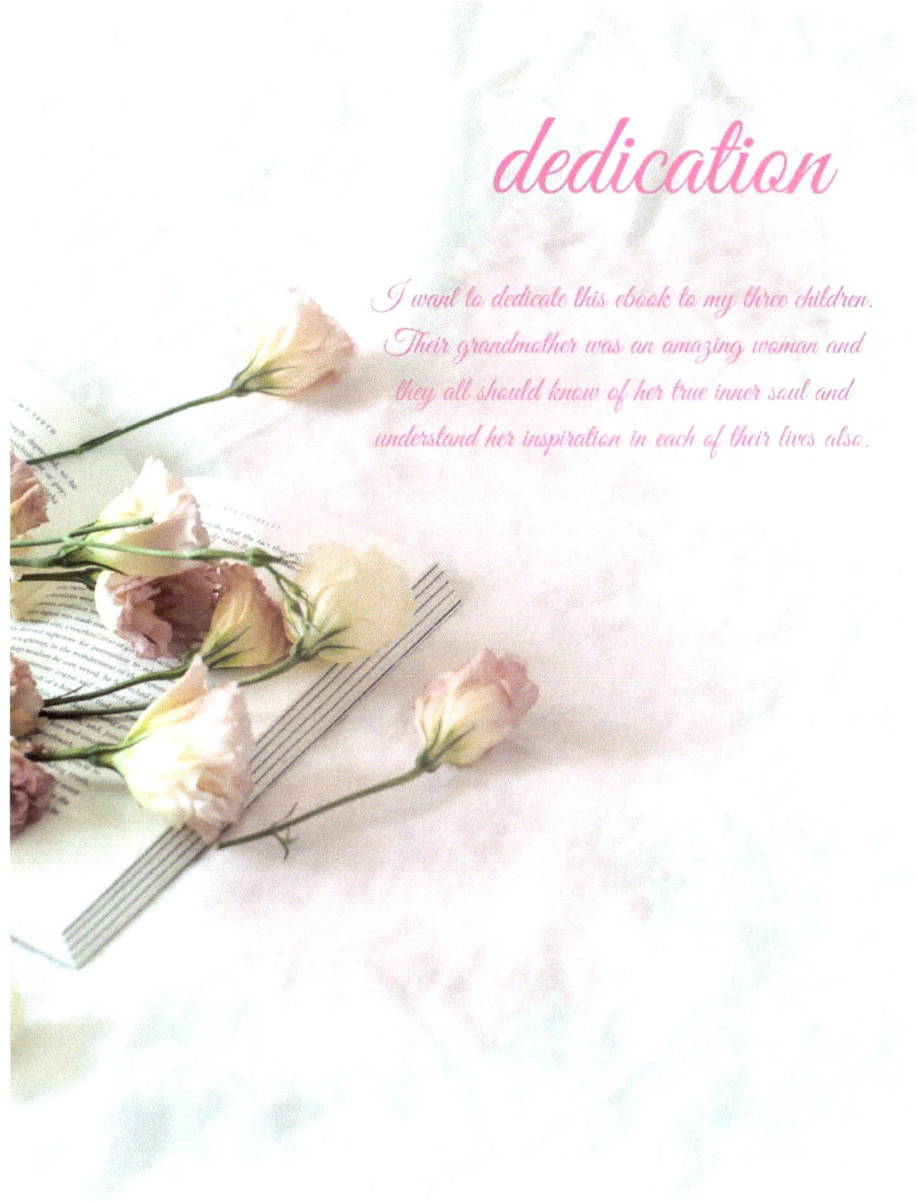

I want to dedicate this ebook to my three children. Their grandmother was an amazing woman and they all should know of her true inner soul and understand her inspiration in each of their lives also.

the author

I am an Acrylic Artist that enjoys painting as much as I can just for the love of expression. I am writing this eBook because I wanted everyone to know just how my mother has been an inspiration to me and my Art Business.

I have learned more than I can tell you from my mother over the years that I had her in my life. But I intend on telling you within these pages just how much my mom means to me and exactly how she is encouraging and inspiring me as well in my Art Business every day.

I am married to a very loving man who has blessed me with three grown children. They all have lives of their own now and sadly only remember very little about my mother. It will always sadden me that they never truly had a chance to know their grandparent on either side.

In these pages I will give you the reasons that I look to my mom for direction and inspiration. I want you to fully understand everything you need to grasp and know as to why I want to carry on my mother's legacy and why she is in every piece of artwork that I create.

She was not only a mom and wife. She was many other things, and no one really knows about those other things. They all have fell into a hidden space that no one knows to go look into after she gained her wings. I believe that once everyone knows about her true inner self that my mom's years of struggles and feelings of insecurity will all be worth the pain that she went through.

Johnanna Barnes / Preshusjnel Art

the author

As you read through this short version of my mom's legacy, you will see that she was similar to all of your mothers and that she was a light to my life. I have taken that unique light of hers and integrated it into my artwork as well and my Art Business. It is because of her and what she has instilled within me that you are able to see and have the chance to own my artwork that brings joy and happiness to you and others in your life!

Because of my mother and her guidance of me and the directions that my art was taking when I was younger, you have the opportunity to experience her heart and well as my inspirations from her and her special way of allowing her art to flow out of her. Enjoy the read and thanks for your interest in my mom's connection to me!

Johnanna Barnes / Preshusjuel Art

table of contents

table of contents (cont.)

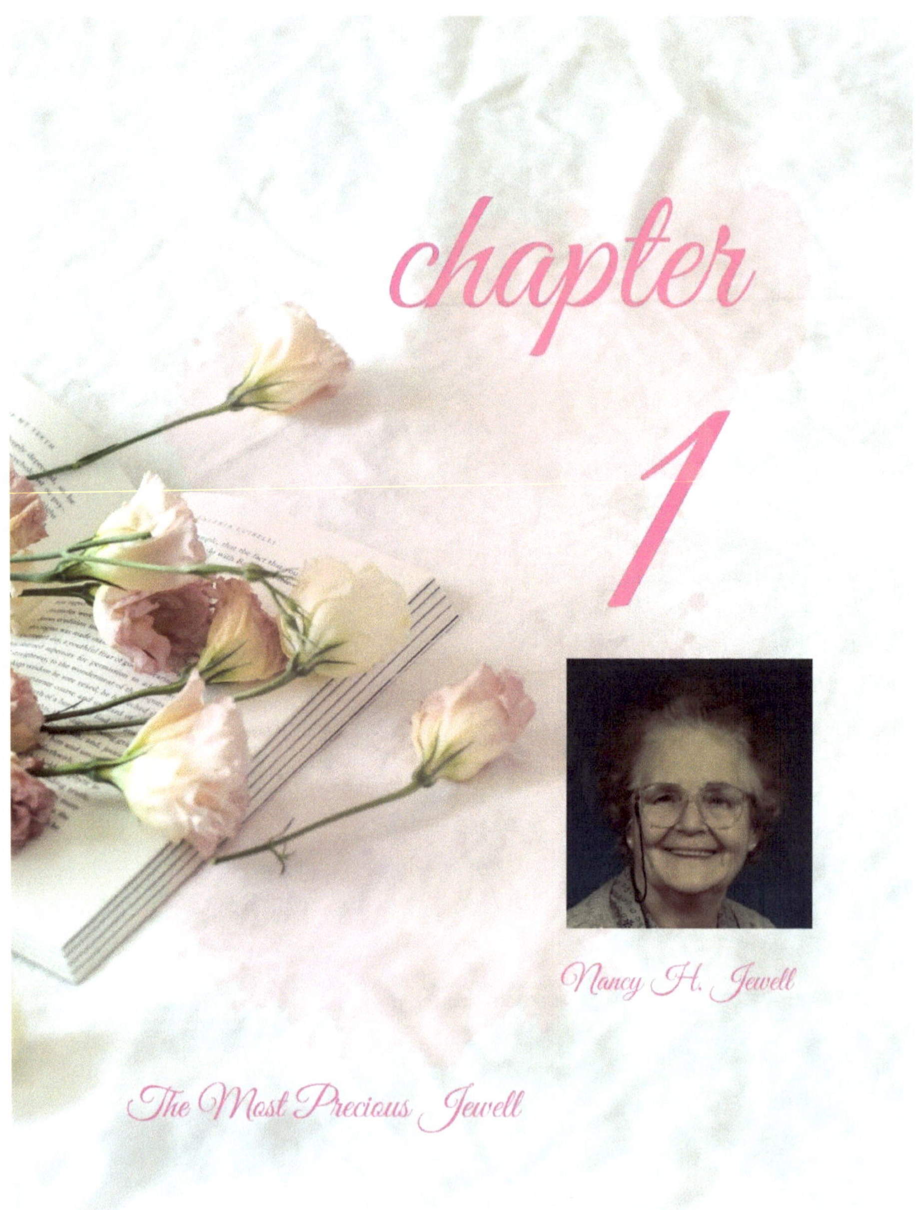
chapter
1
Nancy H. Jewell
The Most Precious Jewell

The Most Precious Jewell

From The Beginning…

To me that is, nowhere even close to what she meant to me!!

For the most part she was just a mother, or just a wife, or even just a Christian. But to everyone that knew her, really knew her she much more than that. So many times, throughout my childhood and formative years she was always the one that I clashed with, the one that I really would rather be away from. She would just have that special knack of knowing just what it took to get under my skin, or even hit that special nerve that changed my whole demeanor as well as personality for any one given day. I know that it is not something that we as adults and even as Christians are supposed to do but at those ages of my life, my flesh did a lot more speaking than God did to me. That still should not be any excuse and I see that now.

For everyone that does not know who I am referring to, it is my mother. She played a very important role in my life that I had now idea of her doing at the time. As I went through my childhood, my mom was the one who was stern and set in her opinions as well as what she thought about everything. She was very intent on telling you about how she felt as well, she did not care how it made anyone feel. Growing up like that was not the best but it was not the worst either. I mean when I think about it, she made sure that us kids always had the things we needed, but a lot of the times those things were not what we preferred to have. Times were hard yes, but there was always love in our family, sometimes that love us kids did not necessarily want to have.

The Most Precious Jewell

From The Beginning.. (cont.)

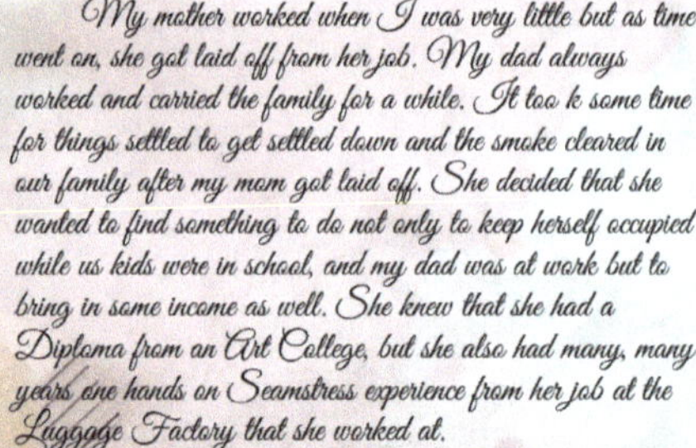

My mother worked when I was very little but as time went on, she got laid off from her job. My dad always worked and carried the family for a while. It too k some time for things settled to get settled down and the smoke cleared in our family after my mom got laid off. She decided that she wanted to find something to do not only to keep herself occupied while us kids were in school, and my dad was at work but to bring in some income as well. She knew that she had a Diploma from an Art College, but she also had many, many years one hands on Seamstress experience from her job at the Luggage Factory that she worked at.

She knew that she wanted to do something that she knew how to do and enjoyed doing as well. She searched around for a while but at the same time she was very diligent in maintaining the house and us kids while dad was at work.

My mother was a person that was always determined at everything that she considered doing. This made us kids look at her as fearless and courageous. At other times we saw her as conscientious and ingenious, but what kids did not see their parents that we when they were going up. Growing up, we thought of her as a normal mother most of the time, but when she was being creative, well then it was a whole other story. She finally felt that almighty urge that we artists all do before long in our lives.

The Most Precious Jewell

From The Beginning… (cont. # 2)

She started her own Seamstress business out of our home. She had my dad help her with creating the sign for the business and when they were done, they mounted it in the front yard, where it hung for many years to come. After helping the neighbors with repairs, alterations, and even sewing creations that they wanted, my mom got restless. The income was not what she wanted or needed it to be for the family. So along with her sewing business she started putting her Art Diploma to good use.

By this time my sisters and brother were grown and either already moved out on their own or about to. I was in high school and being the baby of the family, I was receiving a lot of perks within the family. Those perks included help with my homework when I needed it, firsthand experience in finances, because I had the opportunity to try paying all of the household bills. I did that for well over six years. I also got to hang out with my friends whenever I wanted to and go out every weekend. Another perk was getting my mom to help me in my Commercial Art Class.

A Teacher of Art and Sewing

Johnanna Barnes / Page 12

10

The Most Precious Jewell

From The Beginning... (cont. # 3)

Only one of my sisters enjoy things art related and mom also taught her a few things as well but a lot of what she learned was self-taught or but watching our mother. On the other hand, my brother and sisters had the chance to be in 4-H and Boy Scouts; I never did anything like that because it really did not interest me. I guess you can say that my mom balanced things in our lives at much as she could at the time. But one thing she was very strict about and that was that we ALL had to be Church! It was about the time that I was a sophomore in high school that I remember my mom and one of my sisters were teaching in the Christian School that we had at our church Victory Chapel.

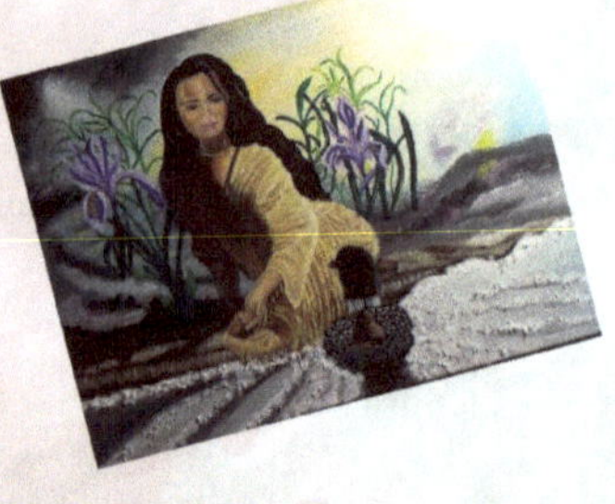

My mom and the staff at the Christian School tried their hardest to convince me to switch my school. But I am being a very rebellious teenager sternly refused only because of one thing and that was because the Christian School could not offer me and Drivers Ed Class. I wanted my license so I could get away from the stresses of being a teenager. But little did I find out years later that those very stresses are what make me who

I am today. My mother was always one to stand with me in whatever I wanted or decided to do, so she did not force me to go there. They taught there for the next two years, and I went on to graduate from high school. I moved away not long after I graduated. One reason was to get away from the authority around me, and the other reason was to explore my surroundings and the world therein.

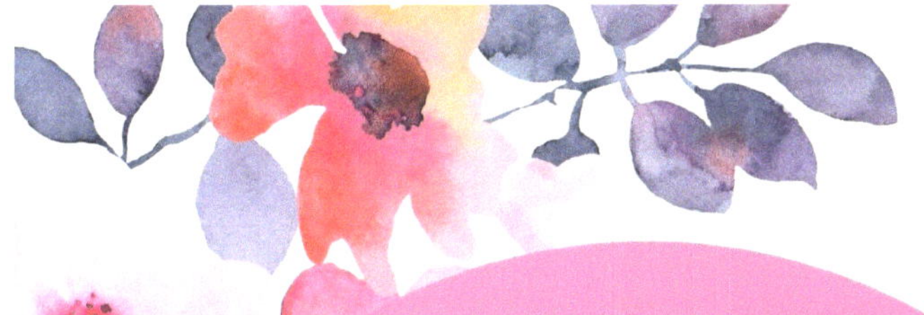

MOM SERVED THE COMMUNITY

Mom was a Craft Teacher at the
Modern Maturity Center in
Dover, Delaware
for over two years, she was also the
Center's Chaplin during that time at
Silver Lake Fishing Club, in Dover, De also.

My Mom loved teaching and helping others which is
probably where I get it from as well.

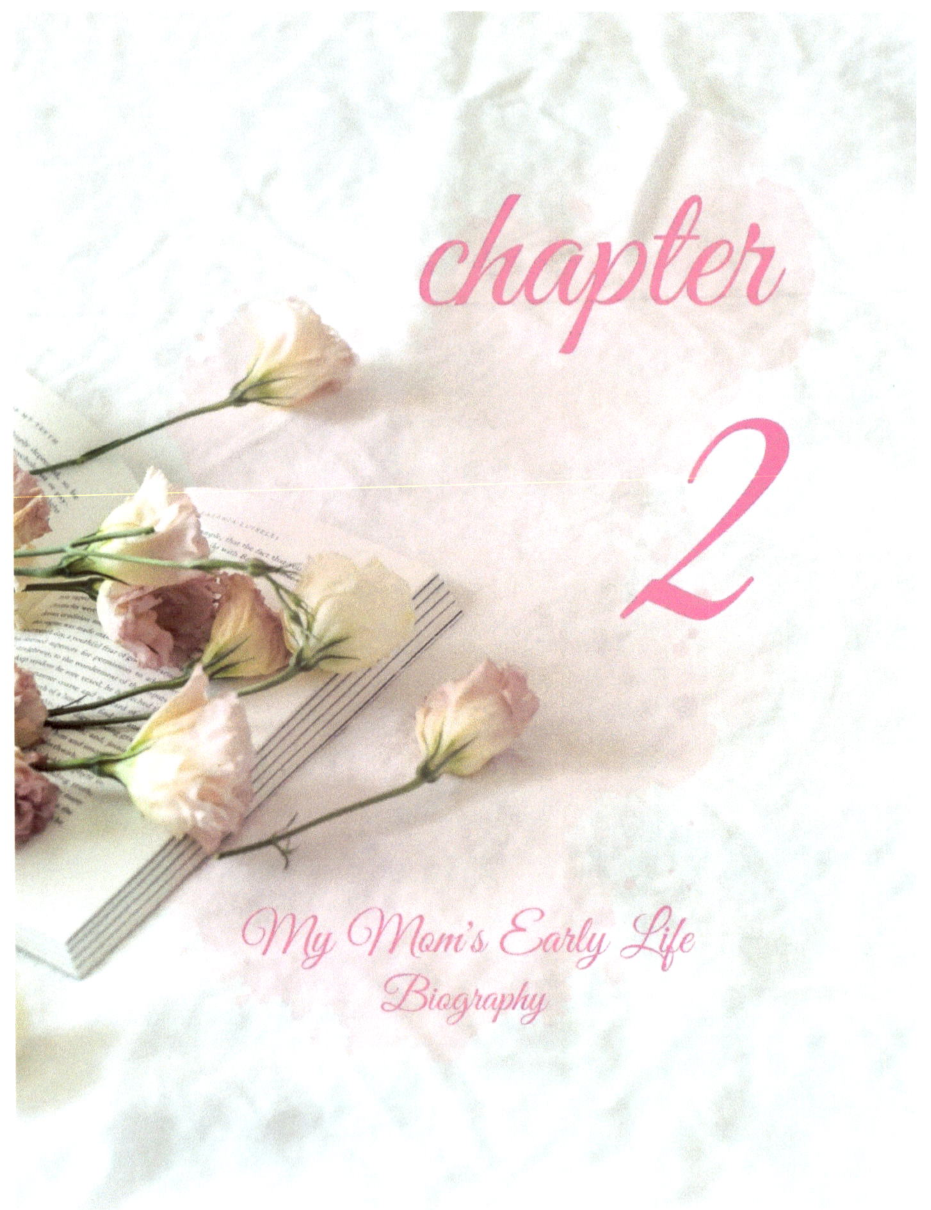
chapter
2
My Mom's Early Life
Biography

Nancy H. Jewell

Biography

Nancy Henrietta Lane was born September 29th, 1928 She Gained her Wings on December 14th, 2 She was born in Philadelphia, Pa. to the late Albert and Bertha Lane.

She was the eldest of 8 children and each one of her siblings looked to her for guidance in tough times they had in their lives. She had to quit school in her formative years of her education to because she had to go to work to help her family get through the worst times of their lives. Being the eldest of all of the children, she of course had to help her mother with the other younger children when she was not working.

She also helped her father as well when she was able to. Her father was the grounds keeper at the nearby golf course. Her mother did not work due to the needs of the children and the home at the time.

The lessons that she learned growing up under her parents stayed with her throughout her entire life. Her first job turned out to be her only job as well. She worked for Leeds Travel Ware as a seamstress before becoming a private seamstress in our home. Nancy was married twice, first to Walter A. Darrell Sr. in 1953- 1963 and then to John Jewell in 1964 until they both gained their heavenly wings.

My Mom's Loom

14

Nancy H. Jewell

Biography... (cont. 1)

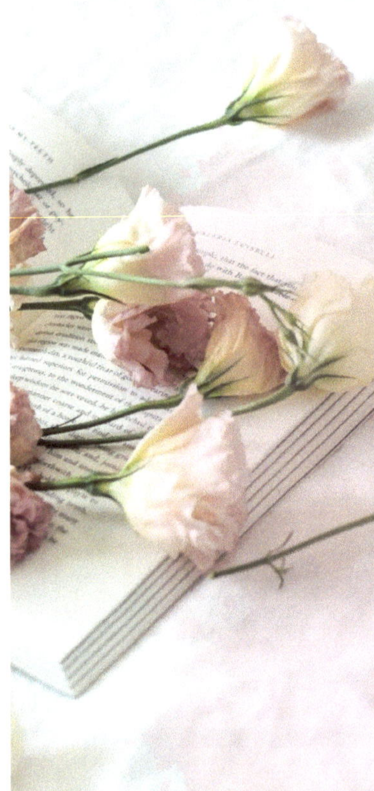

She was first married at a young age to a man that gave her three strong, stubborn and amazing children. Her second marriage produced me, and my three stepbrothers. We all ranged in age of course but all hade that familiar attributes of our parents for sure. Nancy tried her best to spread her love to us all and we each tried her patients very much every day! Even after years of motherhood and being a wife twice over, she still yearned for more in her life. She tapped into the lessons that she had acquired in her younger years. She soon began to allow her creativity to come out in full bloom!

We all ranged in age of course but all hade that familiar attributes of our parents for sure. Nancy tried her best to spread her love to us all and we each tried her patients very much every day! Even after years of motherhood and being a wife twice over, she still yearned for more in her life. She tapped into the lessons that she had acquired in her younger years. She soon began to allow her creativity to come out in full bloom!

Nancy enjoyed arts and crafts and had won several many ribbon awards for her paintings and other works. She had also taught arts and crafts at the Modern Maturity Center and Victory Chapel Christian School both in Dover, De as well as teaching family members.

Nancy H. Jewell

Biography... (cont. 2)

We all ranged in age of course but all hade that familiar attributes of our parents for sure. Nancy tried her best to spread her love to us all and we each tried her patients very much every day! Even after years of motherhood and being a wife twice over, she still yearned for more in her life. She tapped into the lessons that she had acquired in her younger years. She soon began to allow her creativity to come out in full bloom!

Nancy enjoyed arts and crafts and had won several many ribbon awards for her paintings and other works. She had also taught arts and crafts at the Modern Maturity Center and Victory Chapel Christian School both in Dover, De as well as teaching family members. Nancy had also been the Chaplin for many years at the Silver Lake Fishing Club in Hartley, De formerly of Dover, De.

Nancy was a very private person and when she wanted to express herself, she would always look for a new creative way to do it. She crocheted, knitted, sculpted, was a very seasoned seamstress, and she did pottery as well as glass art. She made candles and even made homemade wine.

So, as you can see, she was very well rounded and if she ever found something that she had not tried before that she like or that interested her, she most definitely would give it a try. Some things did not appeal to her after she tried them, but she always gave them her best effort. Nancy always wanted her kids to never give up and always do our best at whatever they were doing. She instilled many moral and conscientious values into all of her children, but sometimes they did not always adhere to those teaching.

i never dreamed

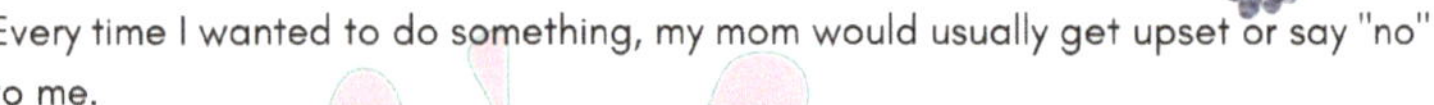

When I was a kid, I never thought that I would be so much like my mother.

Here and I were what seemed like opposites. There were times I thought that I was maybe adopted.

Every time I wanted to do something, my mom would usually get upset or say "no" to me.

- I usually went to my daddy because I was a "daddy's girl".
- My mom never trusted me at my word but believed my lies.
- She never really had an interest in things I liked to do but my dad always did

Even as a teenager I rebelled towards her and that was one of the reasons that I left home.

As an adult though things changed for her and I.

Her and I grew closer after I moved away and got married. I have no idea why but every time we talked, I felt her heart and I knew that she truly wanted the best for me. She was very supportive and helpful to me and when she needed something important, she knew that I would be there if I could!

- She would come to visit as often as she could to visit me and my family.
- It seemed as if time had no moved ahead for so many years and she was the way that I remember her being as I was growing up when she would visit.
- We actually enjoyed each other and enjoy spending as much time as we could together

I realize at this time in my life that the short time that I had with my mom was nowhere near enough time. I miss her more and more every day!

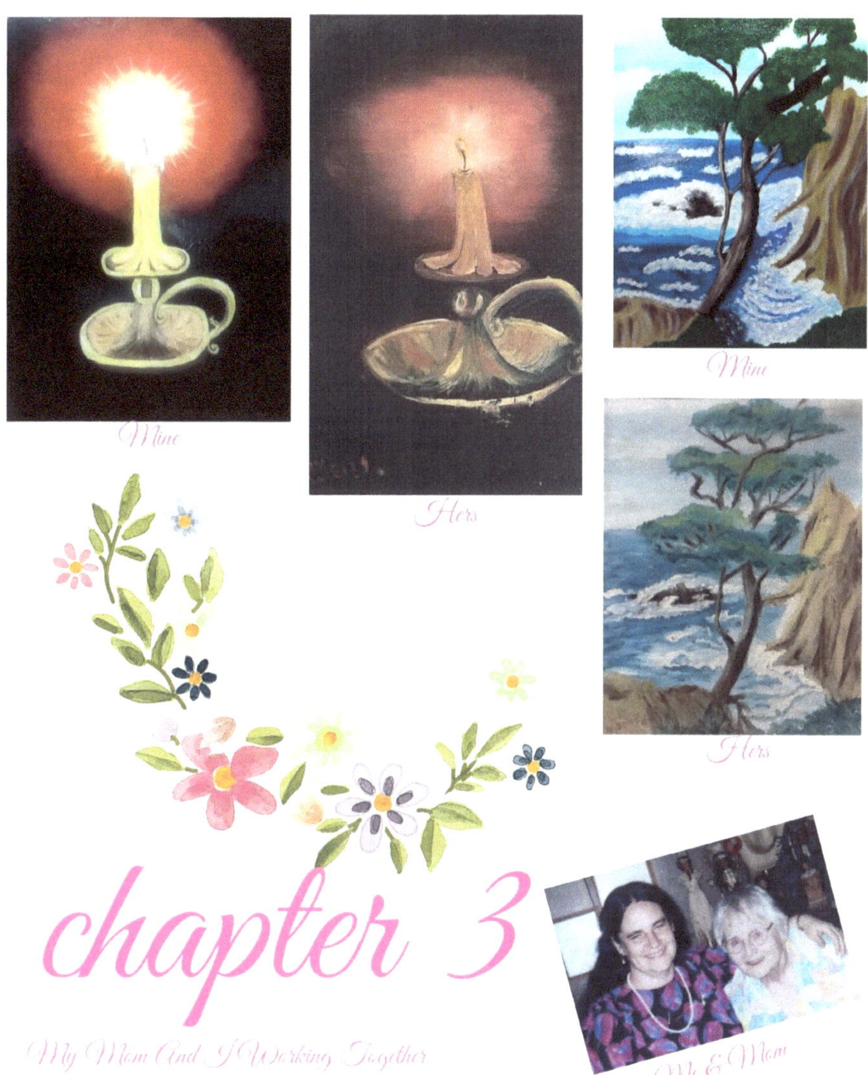

Mine

Hers

Mine

Hers

chapter 3

My Mom And I Working Together

Me & Mom

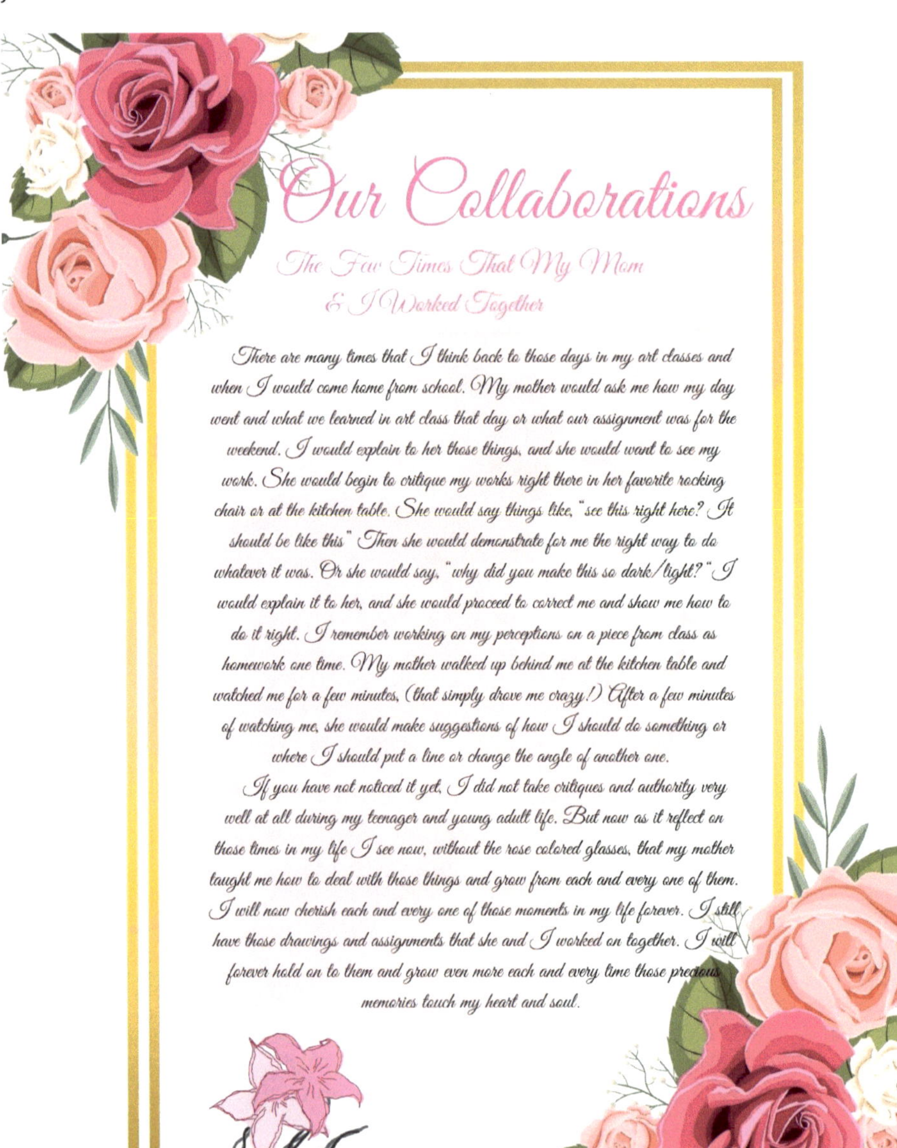

Our Collaborations

The Few Times That My Mom & I Worked Together

There are many times that I think back to those days in my art classes and when I would come home from school. My mother would ask me how my day went and what we learned in art class that day or what our assignment was for the weekend. I would explain to her those things, and she would want to see my work. She would begin to critique my works right there in her favorite rocking chair or at the kitchen table. She would say things like, "see this right here? It should be like this" Then she would demonstrate for me the right way to do whatever it was. Or she would say, "why did you make this so dark/tight?" I would explain it to her, and she would proceed to correct me and show me how to do it right. I remember working on my perceptions on a piece from class as homework one time. My mother walked up behind me at the kitchen table and watched me for a few minutes, (that simply drove me crazy!) After a few minutes of watching me, she would make suggestions of how I should do something or where I should put a line or change the angle of another one.

If you have not noticed it yet, I did not take critiques and authority very well at all during my teenager and young adult life. But now as it reflect on those times in my life I see now, without the rose colored glasses, that my mother taught me how to deal with those things and grow from each and every one of them. I will now cherish each and every one of those moments in my life forever. I still have those drawings and assignments that she and I worked on together. I will forever hold on to them and grow even more each and every time those precious memories touch my heart and soul.

art was handed down

Mom got her Spark from my grandfather

MY GRANDFATHER WAS VERY GOOD AT WHITTLING THINGS OUT OF WOOD.

I would love to go to my grandparents' house when I was little because I would always find something to intrigue myself with. I grandfather had a basement full of all kinds of things he has carved out of wood, for his family and he would spend hours down there working on different projects. We were never4 allowed down there and of course that made it that much more interesting for us kids!

- He carved toys for the kids to play with and ride on.
- He would sit outside and whittle sticks into something useful for the house.
- My favorite things were his large sailing ships and tankers that he carved out of wood. They took him many months to finish.

My grandfather was very sweet and loving. I believe that is where my mom got her first interest in art and crafts.

MY MOM GOT HER ART DIPLOMA AND THEN TAUGHT MY GRANDMOTHER AND AUNT.

The interest in art grew after my mom received her knowledge. She went on to teach my grandmother and my aunt as well because they saw how well she was doing, and it made her so happy. They both wanted to try it and fell in love.

- My grandmother had an entire room full of nothing but her paintings.
- My aunt would always make her own cards all from hand and in 3D
- They both loved to create and were always making something when we would visit them.

Art has even flowed the other way in my family to one of my sisters and my niece

as well.

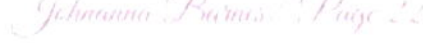

mom's tips...

mom's tip 1
Karma

What you do to others will always come back to you. So always give what you want back.

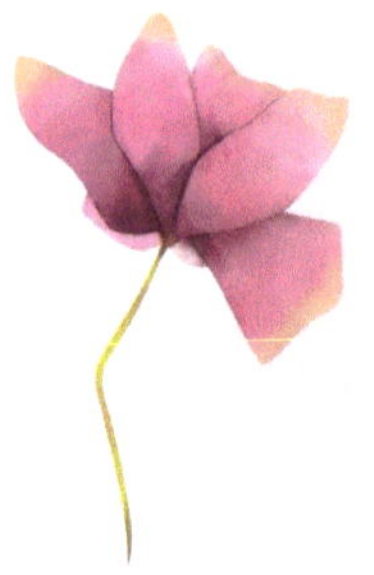

mom's tip 2
Always Give Your Best

Always do a job a job to the best of your ability. Never only give a portion of your ability to others, because you know in your heart and souls that you can do better.

mom's tip 3
Always Be Kind To Others

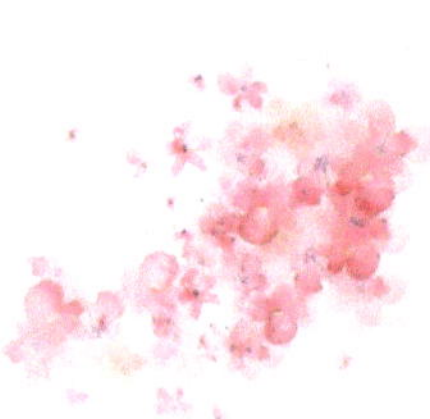

Alwas put your best self out there for others to see and understand that not everyone is mean or cruel and that they could be your best friend, if they are given a chance.

mom's tip 4
Murfy's Law

If anything can go wrong it will, so always be prepared for the devil to throw a wrench into your life. Trust God and allow him to help you know how to deal with it and make it right again!

Johnanna Barnes / Page 23

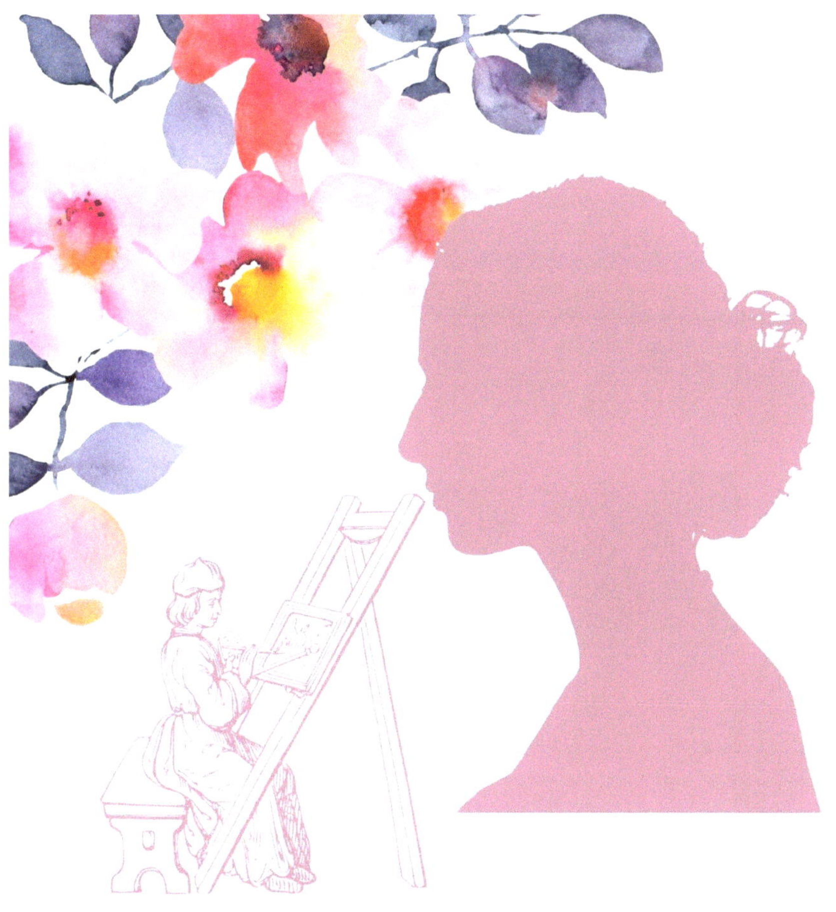

chapter four

Some Things That My Mom Loved

My Mom's Loves

My Mother Was Adventurous At times

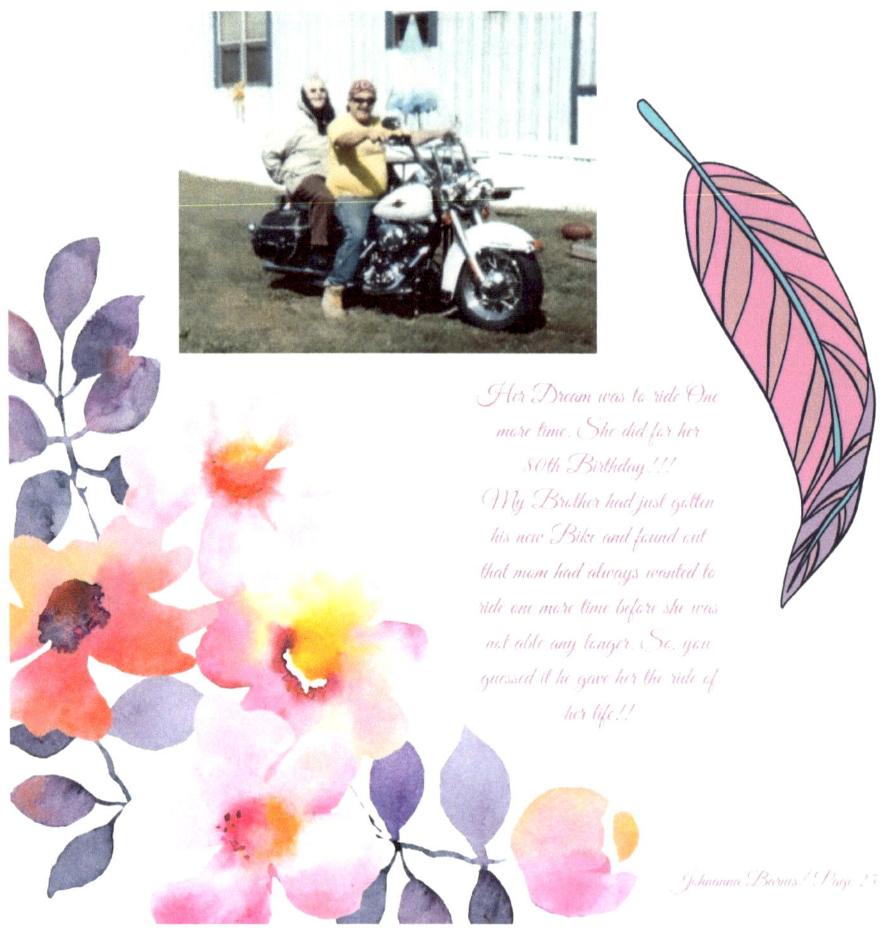

Her Dream was to ride One more time. She did for her 80th Birthday!!!
My Brother had just gotten his new Bike and found out that mom had always wanted to ride one more time before she was not able any longer. So, you guessed it he gave her the ride of her life!!

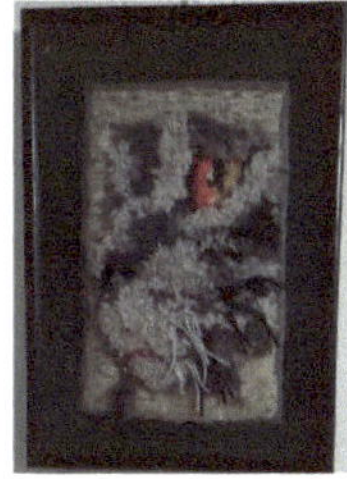
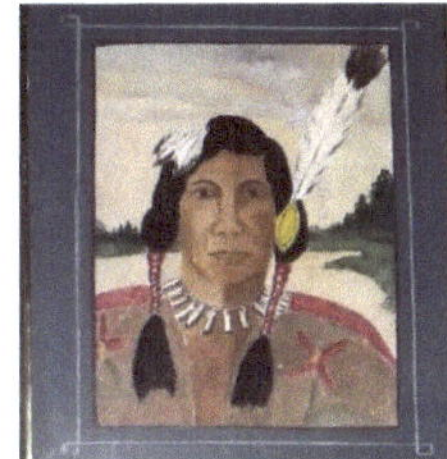
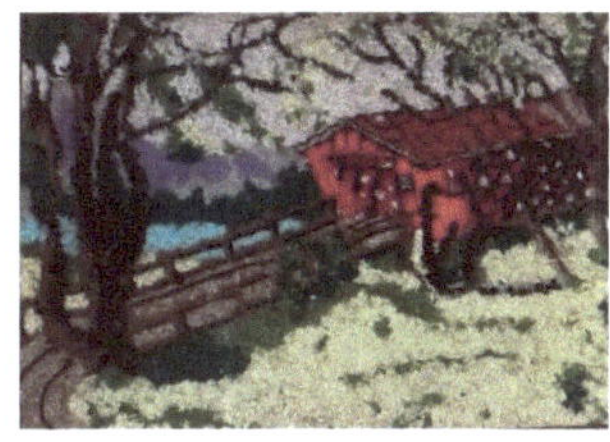
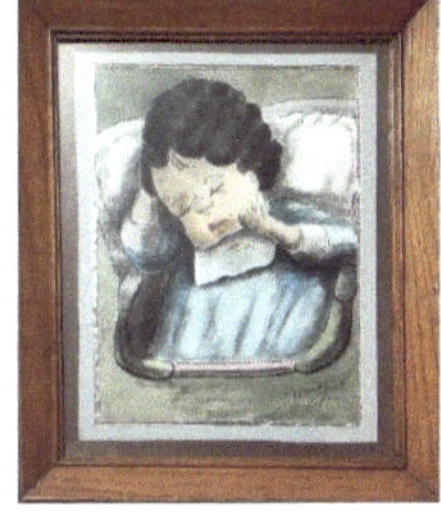
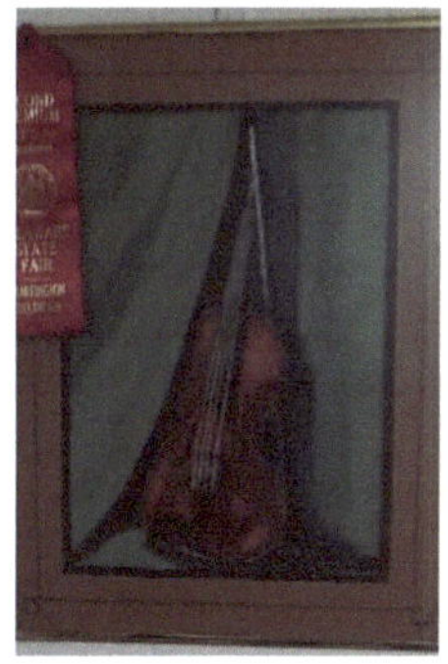

Mom's Artwork

Here are just a few pieces of her work

My mother discovered that she had a love for art was she young; she applied to at Art Instruction of Minnesota. The Commercial Designing course that she that she took there she was able to take through the mail, which worked out great for her at the time. She was able to get all of her assignments and homework done as well as being able to help her family out financially and with her siblings. She managed to get everything done and was able to graduate in In December of 1951.

She held on to that diploma for many years and I still have it to this day. Throughout her life she always knew that she was able to rely on the concepts, ideas, patterns, and even perceptions that that she acquired with it. She did tap into those things as well as many more over the next several decades. She has had the chance to display her work at local Fairs, and Community Centers, a nearby Lodge and as well as even a museum. She has been awarded many Ribbons for 1st and 2nd Place for her artwork and, yes, I have them all as well. She even had her artwork placed on the Front page of a local small newspaper for the anniversary of 911 one year, (I have that also)!! She has pretty much done it all, Crocheted, Knitted, Weaved, sculpted just to name a few. She even created a Woman's Vest to wear that Depicts Our Families Native American Heritage. It had the Honor of hanging in a local Museum as well for I believe over a year, I have it as well)! For many years she would find something to create for Christmas gifts for everyone in our extended family and sometimes even my siblings and me as well. She even made homemade Wine for a few years and used that as gifts. Those were some really crazy years in general, especially with the Sculpted Bust of my father watching over everything in our house!

Johanna Burns   Page 20

mom and the water

She loved being in and around the water, and gave me a love of the water as well!

My mom grew up living near the beach. It was one that I have only heard of when she talked about it and the things that her and her brothers and sisters would do there growing up. It was Woodland Beach, Delaware. I would have loved to at least see photos of it when she lived there but I to this day have yet to see any. I just think that it is more than likely because photos were only something that the rich and famous people were able to do back then.

Woodland Beach as it is today

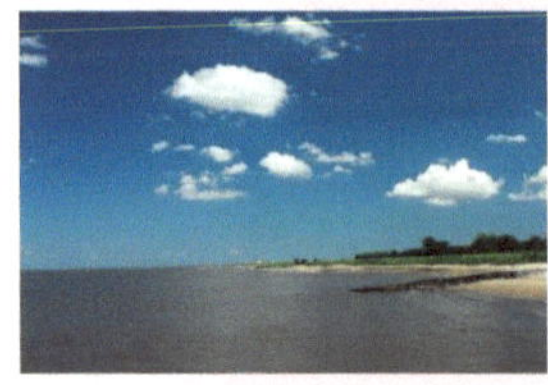

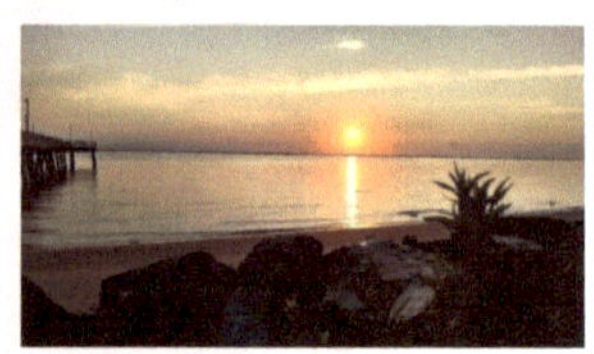

As I was growing up though, our family spent a lot of time at another beach that I do remember very well. We went through good times there; we went through bad times there, it was our "go to road trip spot". It was a time in my life that will never forget and I long for more times than I can count! We even went through a Sandstorm one day there!! This beach has changed more than I care to even think about. It was Betterton Beach, Maryland

Betterton Beach

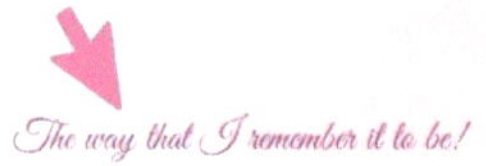
The way that I remember it to be!

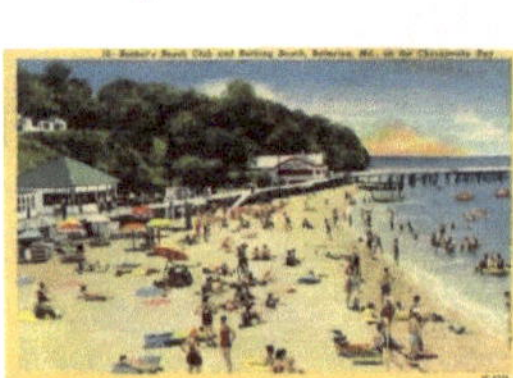

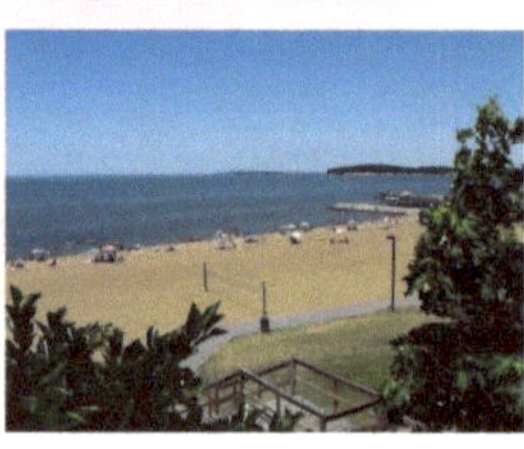

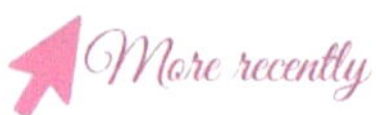
More recently

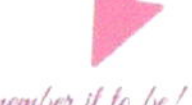
The way that I remember it to be!

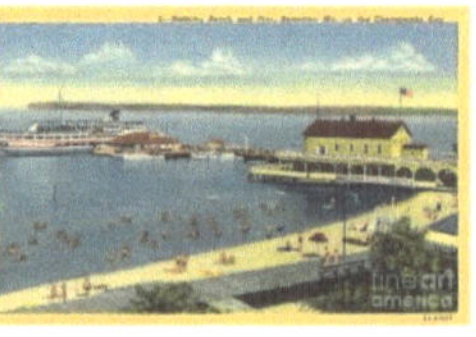

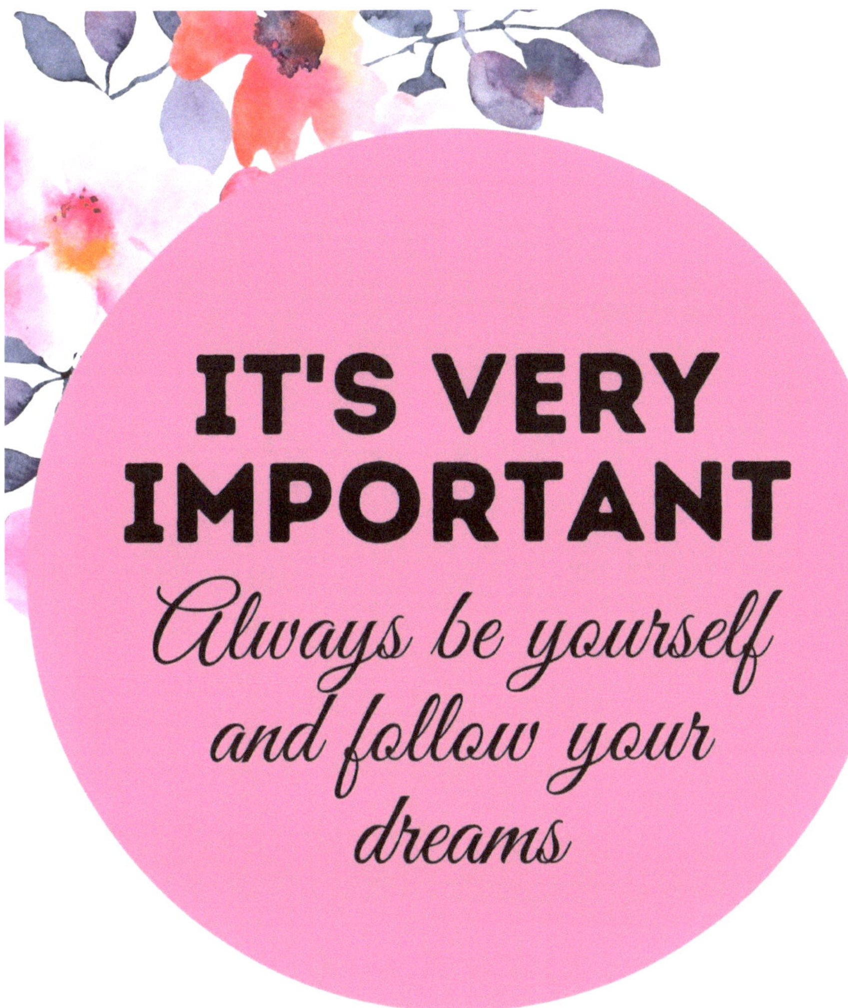

My mom would always tell me this and she drilled into my thought process. I have never forgotten it to this day!

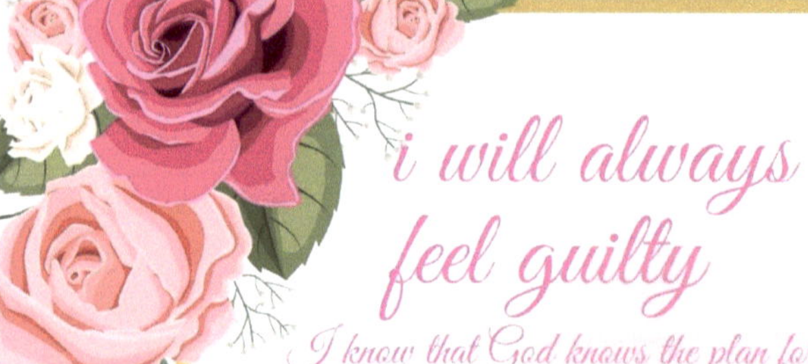

I always wanted to be there for my mother no matter what, like I am sure we all do.

When she needed all of her family the most in her life, I was unable to be there for her. It broke my heart!

- She asked for me to come to her.
- She was fading and wanted to see me before she left.
- I had a car accident and could not go to her.

God blessed her and I to be able to see each other, one last time, before she went home. She held on just long enough to see that I was ok... then she was GONE!!

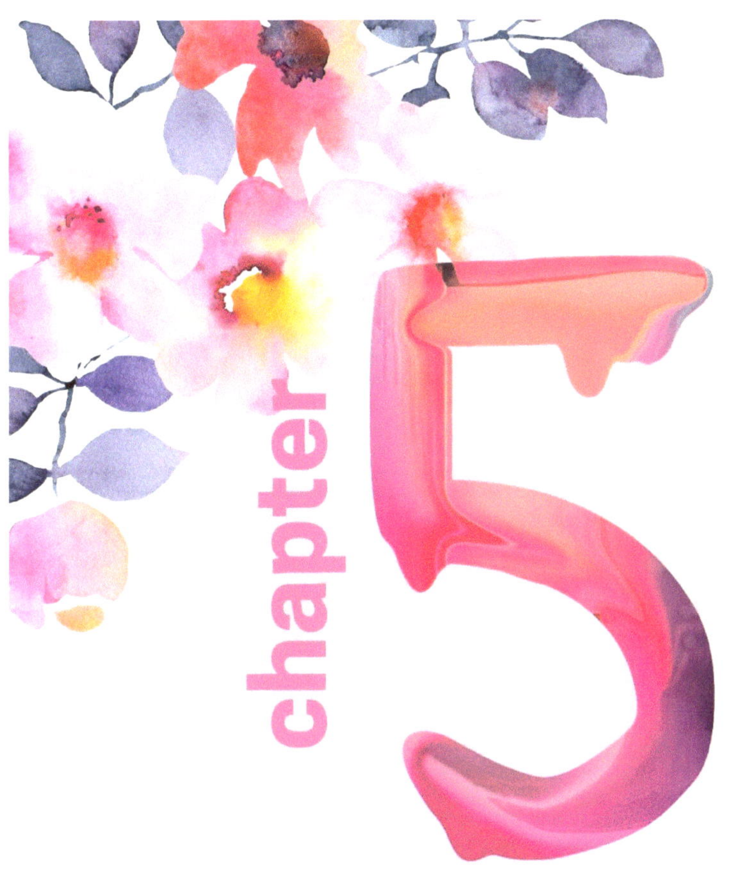

chapter 5

"Everything you can imagine is real." -Pablo Picasso

- Pablo Picasso

our roots
My Mom's Native American Heritage

After I was married and living so far away from my mom and my siblings, mom decided to make a video tape. It was of her heritage and her life along with her accomplishments for each one of her children.

It was like her telling each one of us the things that took place in her life when she was young and all throughout her life as she remembered it. It included her Susquehannock Indian heritage as well, that name meant "Muddy Water People" Which I did not know about until that time. Perhaps that is where she and our whole family get our love of water and being around the water!

It went into as many details of the life and times of the tribe as she could find and remember. It also included how they lived as well as how they were eventually done away with but those people that despised them. In short, they were accumulated of many different tribes that were small in size, and dying off. Still after they all connected and grew together there were only about 20,000 in total That was until they all killed off except the last six. They were sadly killed as well by two brothers who hated them just for who they were.

Mom's Vest

My Mom Handmade This Vest

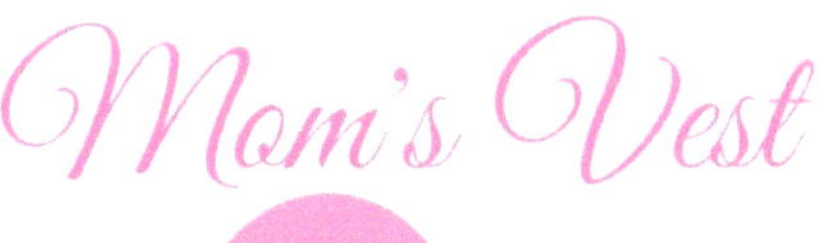

The Front

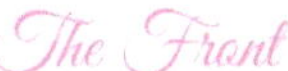

The Back

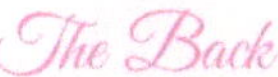

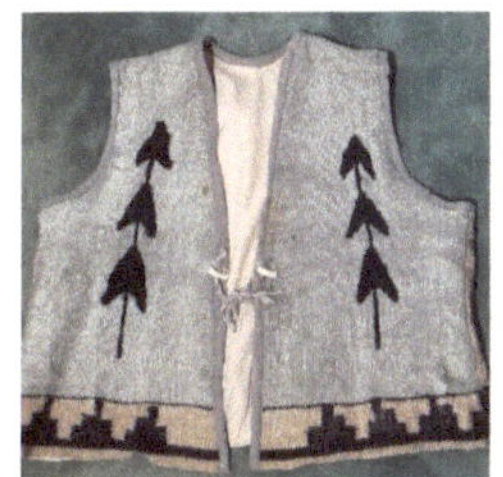

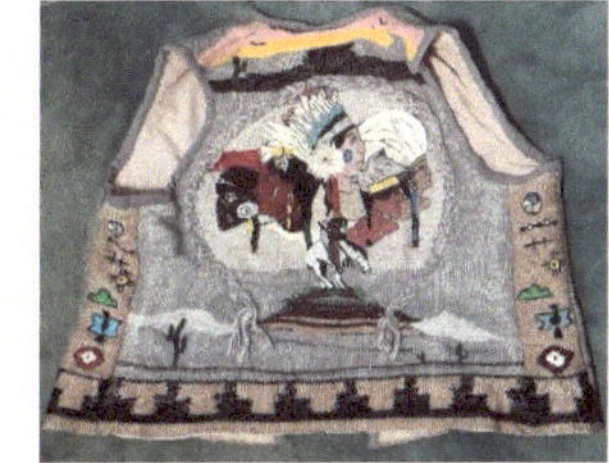

The Center on the Back

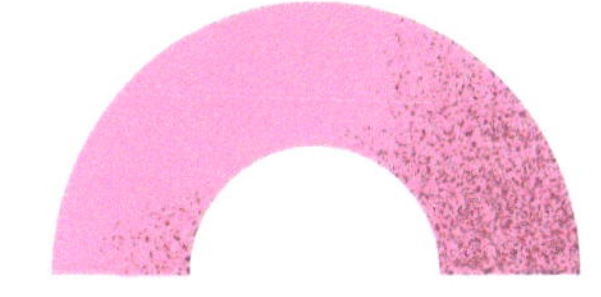

The Sides One The Back

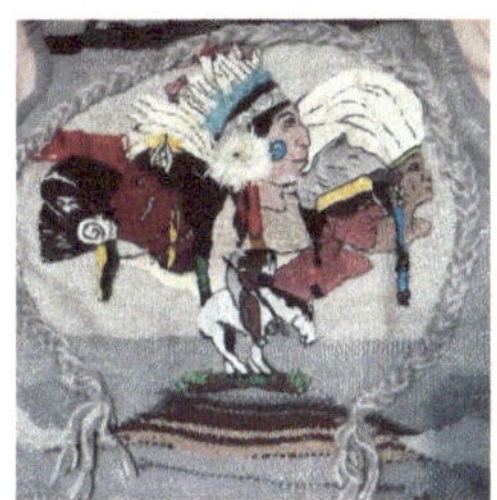

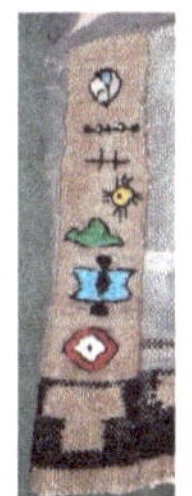

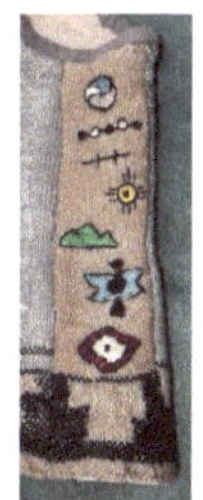

conclusion

No Matter How Much We Try...

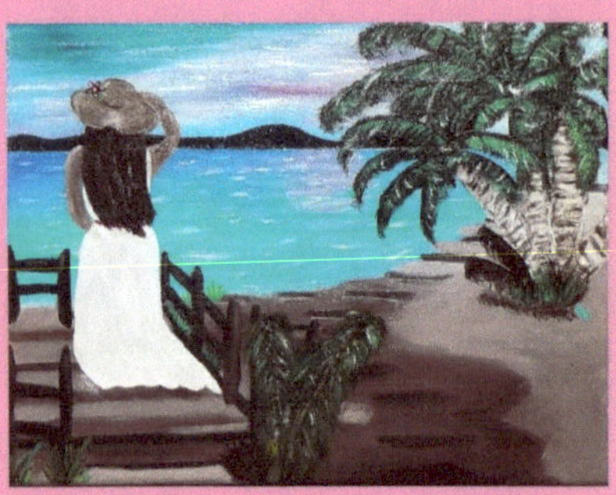

We will always have a love for our parents, and they will always have our best interests in mind for us. We just need to put ourselves aside and pay attention to then while we have a chance.

Sometimes that can be a hard thing to do but God made us in His image, and He knew what things we all would face in our lives. He would never give us more than we each can handle, nor would he leave us in the dangling in the wind without a saftely net.

Just trust in your instincts and intuitions. God gave then to us all for a reason and that reason was not to just ignore them. Trust God to lead you in your life and He will NEVER lead you down the wrong path! I just wish that I would have done that with my mom. If I had all of those years ago, I could only wonder where I would be today and how that simple fact would have changed my entire life!!

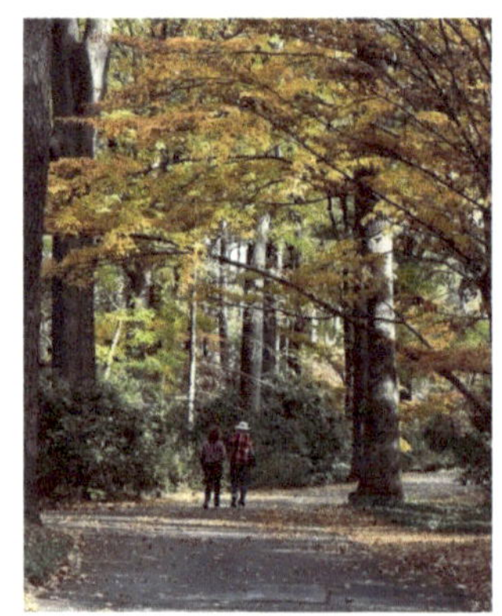

31

I have New Products!!

As time goes by, I am finding a curiosity for new creations!!

I love my artwork and will NEVER leave that! But so much more is out there.

My mom was always looking for something to create. She tried everything that she knew of and even some that she just made up as well.

- She did needlepoint, and pottery.
- She Crotched, Sculpted and even Knitted and made Wine.
- She simply loved being creative. in every way possible.

She never stopped sewing and or teaching how to do things, until she couldn't anymore.

I loved my mother's artwork and will always cherish it all. I see her in all of my own artwork.

I am planning on exploring many new things and sharing them with everyone like my mom did.

- I am an Author and Poet.
- I have eBooks and paperbacks online for anyone that wants to read them.
- I am a Photographer and have taken well over 10,000 photos in my library so far.

I am also working on some NEW Products relating to My Artwork and My Mother. They will be released soon.

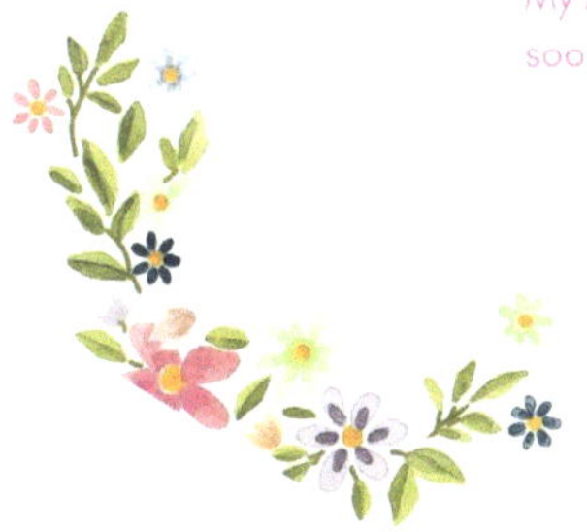

Johnanna Barnes Page 34

always trust in your dreams

Your Future Is Bright So Stay Focused

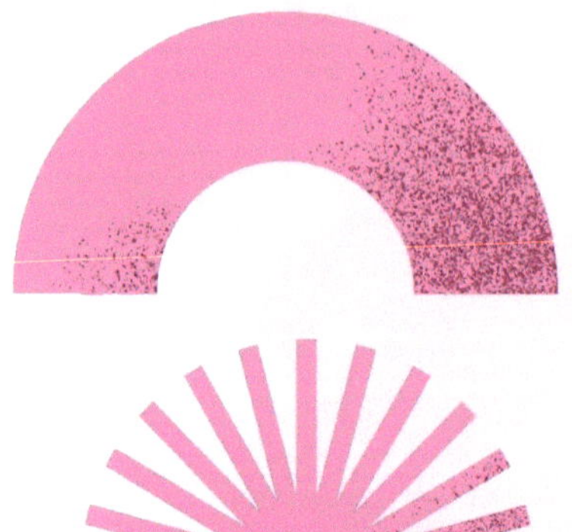

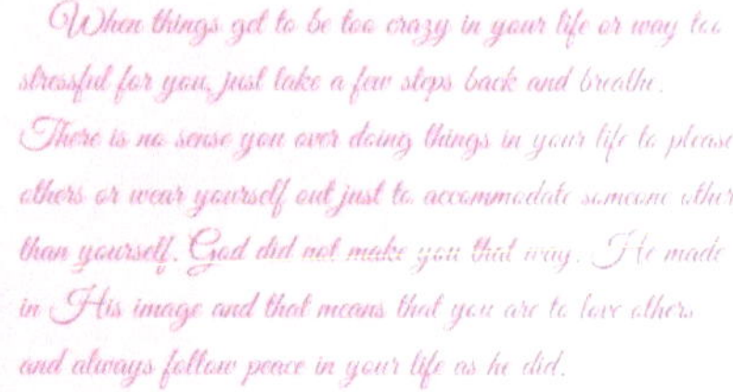

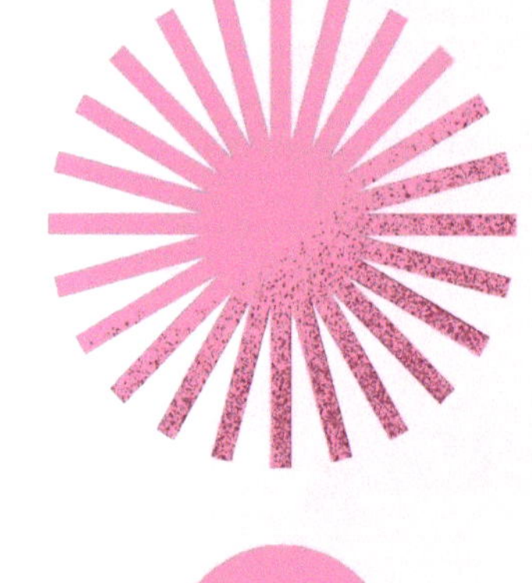

When things get to be too crazy in your life or way too stressful for you, just take a few steps back and breath. There is no sense you ever doing things in your life to please others or wear yourself out just to accommodate someone other than yourself. God did not make you that way. He made in His image and that means that you are to love others and always follow peace in your life as he did.

We all have dreams, and those dreams should always be in the forefront of your life. I mean that is why God gave up dreams and visions. So that we would know what was to come and so we could follow those dreams and visions as long as they are from God, and they bring you peace and love and joy.

My advice is to rest in God and allow his to show you the path and road that you should be on. So not allow other things or other people in your life distract you or detour you from that path or road that you are meant to be on the dreams of your inner soul are usually from God and show you what direction you should go in when you are confused or unsure. God will never lead you wrong. If I had followed my dream of being an artist when I was a teenager, there is no telling where I would be now or how He could have Blessed my life and the lives of my family!!

Johnanna Barnes / Page 33

AFTERWORD

With all of the information I have given you, I know for a fact that there is so very much more to my mother's story. I have tried to gather all that I could to present to you and I can only hope that after you have read these words you have a greater admiration and appreciation for my mother. She was a very unique breed and someone that should not be forgotten by those who loved her or even knew her a little. She walked a straight line but along that line she had fun and loved life and her family She is sorely missed by us all!!